ACCENT ON TWO PIANOS

FOUR ORIGINAL PIECES

BY WILLIAM GILLOCK

ISBN 978-1-4950-2277-7

WILLIS MUSIC

EXCLUSIVELY DISTRIBUTED BY

HAL•LEONARD®

Visit Hal Leonard Online at
www.halleonard.com

Contact us:
Hal Leonard
7777 West Bluemound Road
Milwaukee, WI 53213
Email: info@halleonard.com

In Europe, contact:
Hal Leonard Europe Limited
42 Wigmore Street
Marylebone, London, W1U 2RN
Email: info@halleonardeurope.com

In Australia, contact:
Hal Leonard Australia Pty. Ltd.
4 Lentara Court
Cheltenham, Victoria, 3192 Australia
Email: info@halleonard.com.au

FOREWORD

Although he grew up in rural Missouri, William Gillock's fascination for cultures outside of his own has always been apparent from his publishing output. The titles reflected in this collection are no exception. Gillock traveled nationwide, including to Hawaii, as an adjudicator, but also journeyed abroad to Mexico, Austria, England, and France. The French influence shows up multiple times in his compositions; at least five pieces have "Paris" in the title, and two are included here. Both were published in 1959. (The understated second piano part for "Portrait in Paris" was added in 1971.) "Carnival in Rio" is arguably still as popular as it was when first published in 1969; its lesser-known second piano part was added in 1976. "Viennese Rondo" is cheerful and classically inspired, composed when Gillock was in his early sixties. Its second piano part was published posthumously in 1995.

The first piano parts all stand solidly as solo pieces. Yet Gillock's creation of the second piano enhances the music brilliantly, often unexpectedly, with layers of stunning harmonies and inner voicings.

To Ruth Adele Miller

On a Paris Boulevard

William Gillock

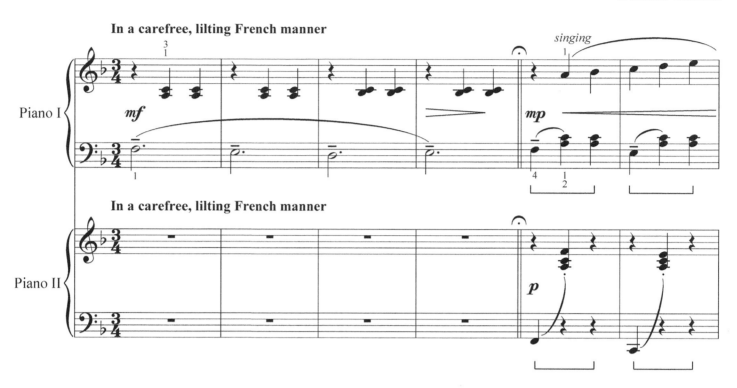

Carnival in Rio

William Gillock

To Beverly Bradley

Viennese Rondo
(Homage to Josef Strauss)

William Gillock

ACCENT ON TWO PIANOS

FOUR ORIGINAL PIECES

BY WILLIAM GILLOCK

WILLIS MUSIC

EXCLUSIVELY DISTRIBUTED BY

HL00146176

FOREWORD

Although he grew up in rural Missouri, William Gillock's fascination for cultures outside of his own has always been apparent from his publishing output. The titles reflected in this collection are no exception. Gillock traveled nationwide, including to Hawaii, as an adjudicator, but also journeyed abroad to Mexico, Austria, England, and France. The French influence shows up multiple times in his compositions; at least five pieces have "Paris" in the title, and two are included here. Both were published in 1959. (The understated second piano part for "Portrait of Paris" was added in 1971.) "Carnival in Rio" is arguably still as popular as it was when first published in 1969; its lesser-known second piano part was added in 1976. "Viennese Rondo" is cheerful and classically inspired, composed when Gillock was in his early sixties. Its second piano part was published posthumously in 1995.

The first piano parts all stand solidly as solo pieces. Yet Gillock's creation of the second piano enhances the music brilliantly, often unexpectedly, with layers of stunning harmonies and inner voicings.

To Ruth Adele Miller

On a Paris Boulevard

William Gillock

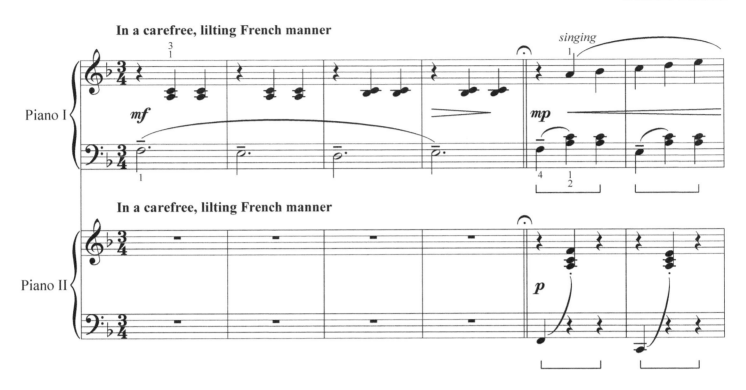

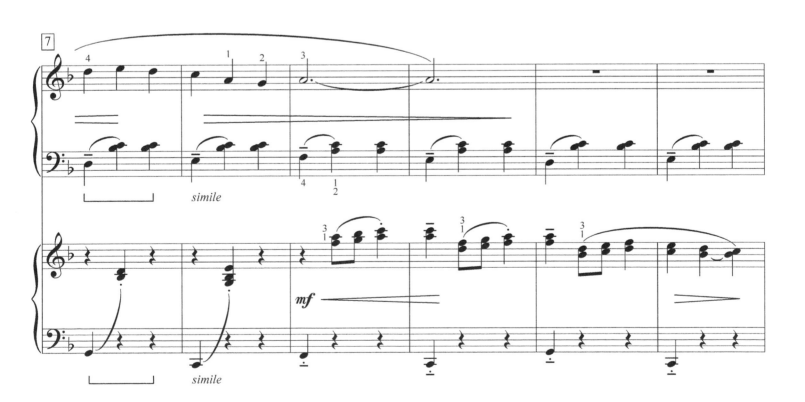

Carnival in Rio

William Gillock

To Beverly Bradley

Viennese Rondo

(Homage to Josef Strauss)

William Gillock

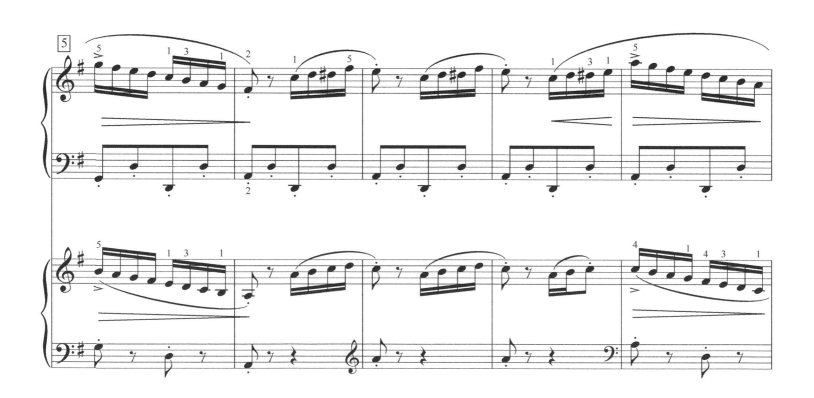

To Earl Jones

Portrait of Paris

William Gillock

With pedal

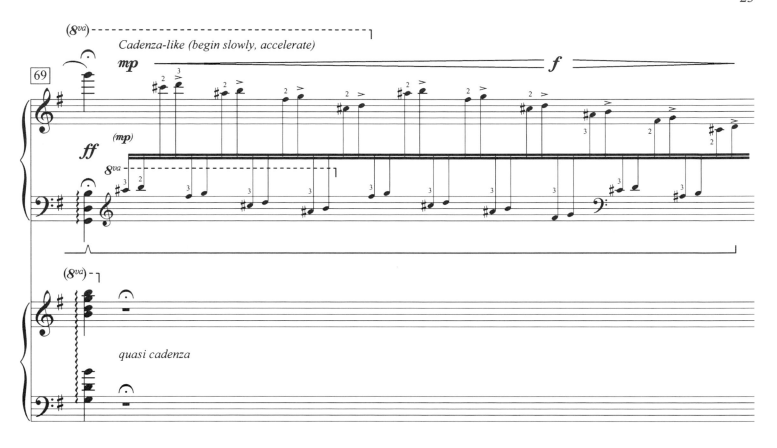

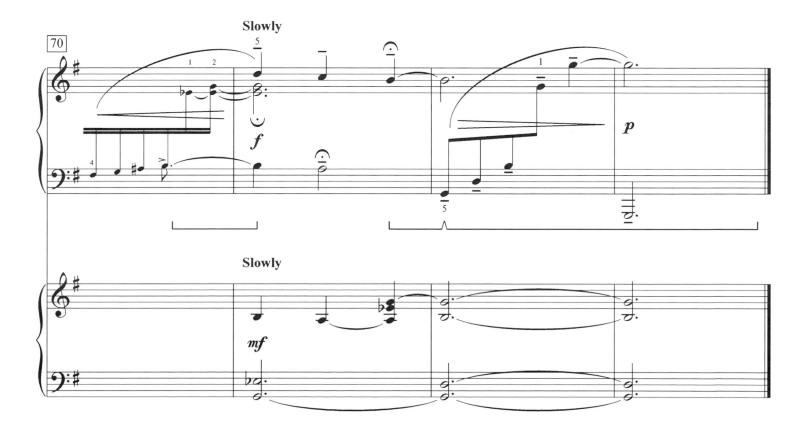

Composer **William Gillock** (1917-1993) once said, "I try

not to write anything that is not worth the effort of learning."

This brief, potent collection for two pianists on two pianos is

worth all the effort in the world. While most of the pieces were

originally written for solo piano, the second piano perfectly complements

the first piano and the results are breathtaking, highly effective ensemble pieces.

Nicknamed the "Schubert of children's composers" in tribute to his melodic gift, Gillock

was born on a small farm in La Russell, Missouri. Although he graduated from college as

an art major, he soon returned to music, his first love, and had much success in his lifetime

as a composer, clinician, and teacher.

To Earl Jones

Portrait of Paris

William Gillock

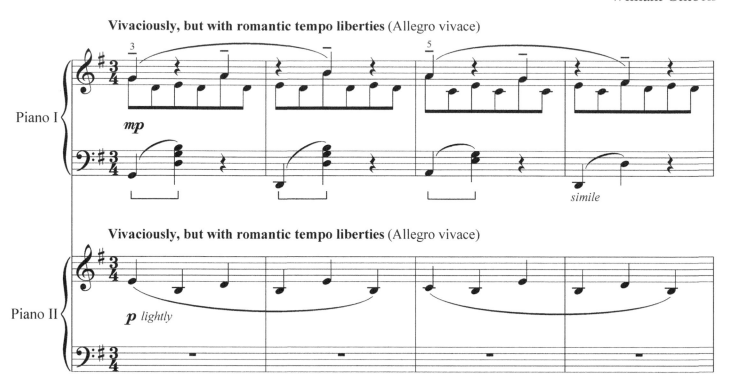

With pedal

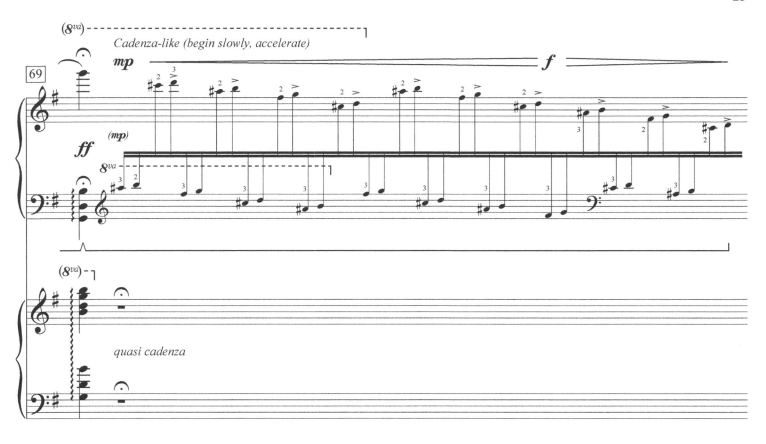

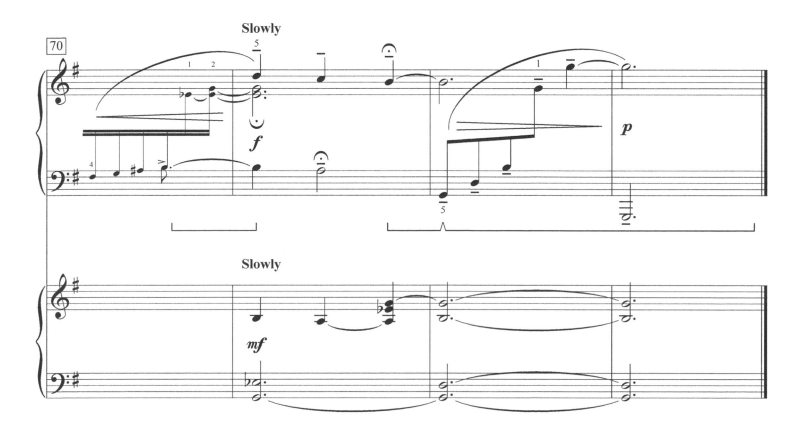

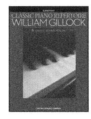

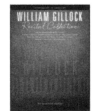